# Lockdown Lines

Helen Davies

# DEDICATION

For my daughter, Isla Pearl
Keep looking for rainbows

# CONTENTS

Lockdown Lines

## The Longest Week

Today we tidied our classrooms,
Like it was the end of the long summer term.
After we wished our students well,
We washed our hands to destroy any germs.

This week has been the longest week,
Full of tissues of germs and tears,
Sanitiser, soap and predicted grades,
Doing our best to allay students' fears.

For once we don't have the answers
For once we're not the experts.
All we know is how we feel,
And this whole thing really hurts.

Let's hope this monster of a virus,
'Does one' pretty quick,
So that the heartbeat of our little community,
Can again begin to tick.


20th March 2020, the day the schools closed

## Goodbye Kenny Rogers

The legend Kenny Rogers has sadly passed away,
He died of natural causes (not COVID-19) his family say.
He and Dolly played at our wedding (not live I hasten to add),
*Islands in the Stream* it was,
Our first dance was so bad.

'We can ride it together, ah ha'.
'We rely on each other ah ha.'

Wise words for these times eh?
Thanks Kenny.


21st March, 2020

## Mothers' Day 2020

Is it Mothers' or Mother's Day?
The debate's the same every year.
Are we celebrating one mother or all mothers?
The apostrophe doesn't matter to her.

Like many of you,
I'm not seeing my mum today.
She doesn't even live that far away (unlike some of your mums).
Let's also remember those mums who are no longer with us,
All those we think of every day.

Social distancing from mum and dad means no Sunday lunch out
at the pub,
No afternoon tea, no hugs or kisses.
But rest assured we'll be facetiming later,
To send all our love and good wishes.

So, Happy Mothers' Day to all our
Mums,
Nannas,
Mothers-in- law,
Childminders,
Aunties,
Carers,
New mums,
Mums-to-be,
Midwives,
The NHS worker mothers,
The supermarket worker mothers,
All the 'key worker' mothers,
We love you all.

Sunday 22nd March 2020, Mothering Sunday

## No work today

I'm not going to work today,
I feel like I'm on the skive.
Just me and Isla at home all day,
We might go out for a drive.

Isla will miss the library and swings,
With nanna and grandad today.
But we have to stay apart from each other,
There is no other way.

Please don't be a covidiot
(I really do like that word)
Stay at home you covidiots!
(the plural sounds more absurd!)

23rd March, 2020

## Biting My Nails

At the age of 45,
the threat of catching coronavirus germs,
has stopped me biting me nails.

I thought about getting a manicure.

But, for now, I think I'll just wear gloves.


24th March, 2020

## 'Fresh' air

'Fresh' air.
O, how we take you for granted.

Granted, the air isn't always fresh
Especially in our big cities.

But I do love the smell of fresh air
It's safe, calm and free.

The exact opposite of how a lot of us feel right now.

Let's hope that all those virus hit lungs
One day soon can breathe in the fresh, spring air.

'Fresh' air.
O, how we will never take you for granted.
Anymore.


25th March, 2020

## People are poorly

People are poorly, we tell out two year old,
The world is suffering from one really big cold.

So we've started painting colourful rainbows,
And we're placing teddy bears in all our front windows.

We can't go to the swings because of a new rule,
We can't go to our lessons at the swimming pool.

We can't go to the cafe, they're cleaning it today,
But what we can do is go outside to play.

What we can do is have a picnic on the grass,
We can play catch and hide and seek and have a right good laugh.

We can make up stories and silly games,
We can play shops and use imaginary names.

We can go for walks and learn to ride our bike,
We can pretend to sing down an imaginary mic.

We can dance and spin and get really dizzy,
We can do anything we like now we're not too busy.

Who really likes soft play centres anyway?!

26th March, 2020

## The First Night We Clapped

Sanitised,
washed,
chapped,
cracked,
All hands in it together.
Clapping.

What a lovely sound as we showed our appreciation,
For the NHS workers across the nation.

I wish we could bottle that amazing sound,
And deliver it to the staff as they do their rounds.


27th March, 2020

## FaceTime Faces

FaceTime faces
Are usually all nostril.
Huge, elongated heads with no bodies.
Bulging eyes.
Monsters!

Unless you get the angle right
It really can be rather disturbing.

(dedicated to all those who are just discovering the power of
FaceTime but who haven't quite got the angle right!)


28th March, 2020

## No spa

So, the spa weekend has been put on hold,
To be honest I'm a little relieved.
My 'bikini body' isn't quite ready,
The 'perfect' look has not been achieved!

So, I'll stick my feet in a bucket,
To reenact the experience at home.
Have a glass of fizz on our patio,
Take a bath with some shower foam.

Put on my old dressing gown and slightly worn slippers,
Imagine a deluxe robe and mules.
Get the paddling pool out and break wind,
My own Jacuzzi and thermal pool.

I'll imagine I'm breathing in invigorating scents,
Not the smell of last night's curry.
I'll imagine there's calming music playing,
Not the sound of my gurgling tummy.

To create my own luxury facial,
I'll put left over cucumber on my eyes.
I'll smother my face in Peppa Pig yoghurt,
Just hope I don't attract the flies.

The spa weekend WILL happen one day
Who knows where, who knows when,
So I'll just keep on imagining,
For as long as it takes until then.

29th March, 2020

## A New Vocabulary

Just checked the OED online
'cause I'm interested in words.
My attention was drawn to 'bearded lady'
It's definitely a new type of 'bird'.

How ironic that 'man-hug'
Now appears in the OED concise.
When we all have to keep away from each other,
Two metres to be precise.

No sign of 'social distancing'
I hope that 'covidiot' is added soon,
Nor can I see 'self-isolating'
The next update is due in June.

'Herd-immunity' appears though
Which actually links to cattle.
I felt like a right cow at Tesco
As I prepared to go into battle.

Here's a couple of others for you to search for,
If you're interested that is.
Have a look for 'coulrophobia', 'puggle' and plenty more,
You could even do the quiz!


30th March, 2020

## <u>A Sonnet for 'Him Indoors'</u>

Happy Anniversary to 'him indoors'
That term is so relevant right now.
These new social distancing laws
Mean it's time to test our vows!

Happy Anniversary to my 'other half',
Whatever that means.
Does it mean that half of me is half of him?
That's certainly the way it seems.

Happy bronze Anniversary to you Paul,
Thanks for tolerating my OCD.
I wasn't sure what to buy you at all,
You deserve a gold medal for being with me.

Thanks for marrying me eight years ago today.
Thanks for making me smile every single day.

(dedicated to my husband Paul on our 8th wedding anniversary)

31st March, 2020

## Hair

I was supposed to be having my hair done this week,
It's usually a nice treat.
To sit down, relax and gossip,
In Zoe's big, black, twirly seat.

But instead I have to face facts,
I'm slowly going to go grey.
And my hair will be down to my shoulders,
Probably by the start of May.

So, what I want to say is this,
I'm embracing the 'au naturel' look.
If anyone dares to say anything,
I'll look like I don't give a...toss!

Old English sheepdog, Cruella de Vil,
Whatever they call you behind your back,
Be thankful it's not to your face (roots),
Never let your poker face crack.

So either do it yourself, shave it all off,
Or cover the roots up today.
But be safe in the knowledge if you did get it done,
No one's going to see it anyway.

(dedicated to all the wonderful hairdressers and colourists
 out there. Our hair misses you and so do we!)

1st April, 2020

## Thursday

It's Thursday!
The new best day of the week!
'Cause tonight we go out!
Not out out.
But, out!

We stand on our doorsteps,
Breathe in the night air.
Our hands have a wild party,
As they clap like they don't care.

We get chance to see our neighbours,
Who have been hiding behind closed doors.
It's like a little street party,
As we join together, one huge applause.

Tonight's night out is cheap, no taxi fare,
There's no need to worry about what you should wear
(joggers or pyjamas both fine).
You don't need to worry about doing your hair,
Just be there, clap and show you care.

Happy Thursday everyone! #clapforourcarers

2nd April, 2020

## A Deadly Infection.

A deadly infection
A disease driven by ignorance.
A virus out of control.
Spreading fear and hate.

Let's make America 'great' he stated,
Free from what he calls the 'Chinese virus'.
His ego multiplies like a deadly killer,
with a gun from a store considered 'essential' business.

His mouth needs washing out with sanitiser.
If there's any left.

3rd April, 2020

## Friends

I'd planned a day in Manchester today,
With my oldest mate.
Our usual routine of shopping,
Followed by a lunch date.

Instead of drinking cocktails at noon,
I'll have a cup of tea.
Instead of lunching in a nice restaurant,
It's a simple sandwich for me.

So, here's to you Caroline,
My wonderful friend for life.
Let's look forward to the next time,
Without all this worry and strife.

Now, the most important thing I want to say,
Check in with friends and family, those who live away,
Send them a message, call them for a chat,
You'll never know how much they really appreciate that.

4th April, 2020

## NCT Mums

There's a group of amazing ladies I know,
In a group we call 'NCT mums'.
We set it up before we gave birth,
When we all had really big tums!

Now we have little people who know their own minds,
Our careers have taken a different direction.
The most important job for all of us now,
Is being a mum, offering affection and protection.

Some are 'key workers' in these testing times.
But it's those who work for the NHS who are the focus of these lines.
So, Suzie and Patsy, this is particularly for you,
To say thank you from the bottom of our hearts for all that you do.

5th April, 2020

## One Sunny Day

A sunny day staying at home,
Is like a football ground without the fans.
Quiet. Empty. Strange.

A sunny day staying at home,
Is like a school with no children.
Quiet. Empty. Strange.

A sunny day staying at home,
Is like a park with no families.
Quiet. Empty. Strange.

But one sunny day soon,
We will return to our favourite places.
Bustling. Overcrowded. Ordinary.

Football grounds will be raucous,
Schools will be buzzing with knowledge,
Parks will be overflowing with laughter,

One sunny day soon...

6th April, 2020

## The Present Participles of Lockdown:

Tik Toking
Crafting
Baking
Painting
Writing
Eating
Playing
Gardening
Tidying
Singing
Reading
Home-schooling
Dancing
Decorating
Laughing
Working
Smiling
Queuing
Sanitising
Washing
Drinking
Zooming
Virtual quizzing
FaceTiming
Scrolling
Re-connecting
Talking
Listening

Pausing.

Stopping.

Thinking
Over-thinking

Reflecting
Appreciating
Noticing
Caring
Worrying
Sharing
Clapping
Thanking
Crying
Reassuring
Praying

Hoping.

Hoping that this storm will soon pass.

7th April, 2020

## Through the Eyes of a Child

I'm not sure what's happening right now,
But I know I'm being protected.
I'm not sure what the news means,
But I know we're all affected.

Even though they've got work to do,
Mummy and Daddy are at home all day.
It's great to spend time together,
Because they always have time to play.

I can't understand why mummy's not rushing me,
I wear my pyjamas, don't get dressed for hours.
We eventually get ready and go out for a walk.
We look for rainbows, listen to birds, pick flowers.

I miss going out and seeing my friends.
I miss going to the park, eating ice cream in a cone.
I miss going swimming and I miss the swings.
I miss cuddling my grandparents; it's impossible by phone.

But we've started this new weekly game,
Where we all stand outside our front doors.
I'm not exactly sure of its name,
But we give one massive applause.

I heard some great news the other day,
The Easter Bunny is free to roam!
She's bringing chocolate eggs to everyone,
But only if we all stay at home.


8th April, 2020

## We have never been so connected

We have never been so connected,
Even when we are so far apart.
Even now, when we're disconnected,
Generosity warms our hearts.

We have never been so connected,
We can do virtually anything these days.
Virtual meetings, virtual workouts,
Virtual pub crawls, virtual plays.
Virtual movie nights, virtual musicals,
Virtual festivals across the bay.

We took part in a virtual pub quiz on our street last night,
Our neighbour's brother was the host.
We finished in third place out of twenty two,
We're not sure who scored the most.

When everything's reconnected,
When society starts to breathe once more.
Let's hope we all become more connected,
Than we've ever been before.

9th April, 2020

## Grief from a Distance

No hugs, no kisses, no whispered words of love,
No stroke of forehead, hand or hair,
No wiping away tears from another's eyes,
Only some reassurance that they know you care.

Putting a brave face on because that's what you do.
Not knowing when and how the funeral will take place.
Not knowing if 'close relatives only' will actually include you.
Preparing for the inevitable.

Console yourself with the knowledge that they know,
Just how much love you all feel,
They want to tell you that this is harder for you than them,
And tell you, that, in time, you'll heal.

Grief is hard enough,
But grief from a distance is even more tough.
Thinking of two close friends at this difficult time,
You are the inspiration for this rhyme.

(dedicated to Dave and Naomi and both your families)


10th April, 2020

### **If you go down to the garden today…**

If you go down to the garden today,
There's an egg hunt taking place.
Make sure you search high and low,
Look in every available space.

You see, while you were sleeping in your bed,
The Easter Bunny was busy working all night.
So if you're lucky today you'll find a lovely little treat,
Which she's carefully hidden out of sight.

But don't forget that once you've eaten all those yummy eggs,
When you've got chocolate all over your face and hands.
Make sure you brush your teeth extra hard before bed,
Or the tooth fairy will have to visit earlier than planned.

Talking of little fairies, watch out for them too,
They are waiting in the garden to spend some time with you.
If you're lucky to find one when you're on the hunt for treats,
Offer them some of your chocolate- it's what they love to eat.


11th April, 2020
Easter in lockdown

## Easter Sunday

Today, the faithful will log-on or tune in
as the The Archbishop of Canterbury delivers his Easter sermon,
by video,
from his flat.

Behind closed doors,
only music will glide peacefully
through the silent aisles
of Notre Dame
in Paris.

Congregations will gather in the sunshine,
to worship on balconies.
The Pope will once again describe doctors and nurses as saints
in Rome.

Drive-thru worship
will take place
across America.

Faith.
La Foi.
La Fede.

Whatever your language.
Whatever it means to you.
Faith.
We need it now more than ever.

12th April, 2020

## **Emptiness**

Deserted motorways,
Quiet streets,
Lonely canals,
Solitary promenades.
We are giving them time to breathe.

Unpeopled beaches,
No tourists swarming outside palaces,
Abandoned woodland,
Parks silent, apart from the sound of nature.
We are giving them time to breathe.

Weeping hearts missing loved ones.
That empty feeling inside
Grief, loss, sadness and pain.
Just breathe. Just breathe.

There's a lot of emptiness in the world right now,
But all of these places will again be full.
Busy, crammed, overcrowded.
No space to breathe.

But hearts will never stay empty.
Because they are brimming with memories.
They are crowded with love
They are overflowing with life.
They give us a reason to breathe.

13th April, 2020

## The Rise of the Naturalist

Naturalists (not naturists),
Are jumping for joy it would seem.
According to a report I saw,
Live from The Forest of Dean.

You see, the sound of nature is on full blast,
Because we've turned our volume down,
People now notice nature's noises,
In both countryside and town.

Noise pollution is decreasing,
So the dawn chorus dominates.
Swifts will return at the end of this month,
To build a nest with their mate.

It might feel like we're on Big Brother,
As nature thrives anew.
So as we make new friendships with neighbours,
Let's make friendships with nature too.

14th April, 2020

## <u>Writing letters</u>

The days of sending letters seem to be a thing of the past,
Compared to texts and emails it's nowhere near as fast.
But there seems to have been a resurgence of penning something by hand,
As we think of different ways to spread love across the land.

The Queen sent Maundy money by Royal Mail this year,
What a break in tradition for her.
The 188 recipients are all over seventy and in self-isolation,
But Covid-19 will not stop them being celebrated by the nation.

I wonder how many people await the arrival of the mail,
Try to work out whose writing or the postmark's trail.
Or listen for the clanging of the metal letter box,
It's even better when the post man or woman actually knocks.

When was the last time you wrote a letter?
Maybe write one to a loved one to make them feel better.
No need to wait for a reason or a special date,
There doesn't need to be anything to celebrate.

In May 2007 I received the most important letter of my life,
From the man who eventually asked me to be his wife.
It came out of the blue and left me overwhelmed with emotion,
But I'm thankful he wrote it; it put our future in motion!

I guess that's why I rate letters so much,
Because the one I received meant so much.
Because that one very special handwritten letter,
Certainly changed my life for the better.


15th April, 2020

## Captain Tom Moore

Physically frail but a giant of a man,
A broken hip but a huge heart,
Walking is difficult for him now,
But he still wants to play his part.

He served in India and Burma,
During the Second World War,
A far cry from Keighley,
where he was born Tom Moore.

He wears his medals with pride; a true champion to us,
As the donations keep coming for the NHS.
What an achievement for this wonderful man,
12 million pounds so far, not a penny less (at the time of writing this!)

He has never stopped serving his country,
This time it's with his walking frame,
He's still serving us now,
As he does laps of his house in Marston Moretaine.

Unlike in 1920 when Tom was born,
Today we are too quick to use words to adorn,
To decorate people as inspirations, legends, heroes,
But all of the above can easily describe this man born...

Tom Moore.
A son.
A dad.
A warrior.
A captain.
A grandad to us all.

16th April, 2020

## **Lockdown continues…**

Look on the bright side,
More memories to make,
More cups of tea,
More cakes to bake.

More Thursday nights out,
Cheering and clapping,
No Sunday night blues,
More afternoon napping.

More lessons with Joe Wicks,
More crazy family times,
More bingeing on Netflix,
More of my daily rhymes.

More time to appreciate,
The little things you adore,
Not worrying about being late,
Or what you look like anymore.

Look on the bright side,
And when the end is in sight,
Remember how you felt right now,
And how we all seemed to unite.

17th April, 2020

## Discovering Zoom

We're doing a Zoom thing with friends this morning,
So I'm planning what to wear,
I'm going to put some make-up on,
And I'm considering washing my hair.

Will be nice to see all their smiling faces,
All at once on the same screen,
We can catch up on all the places,
To which we haven't been!

More important than that though; we have a history,
We've seen each other through the highs and lows you see,
So as we zoom from across the UK to down under in Sydney,
I'm reminded just how special these ladies are to me.

After we've done our zoom thing,
We'll get back to our lockdown routine,
But with a smile on our faces,
Because of the friends we've seen.


18th April, 2020

## You are not alone

There's a lot of wondering,
worrying,
hoping,
In the world right now
Lots of questions:
Why, when and how?

Wondering how you will get through the day,
Worrying where the money will come from,
Hoping others will get in touch.

Wondering how many more millions Captain Tom will raise,
Worrying what today's news will bring,
Hoping you'll sleep tonight.

Wondering when life will get back to normal,
Worrying about your friends and family,
Hoping your planned treatment will begin,

Wondering what day your baby will be born,
Worrying if that cough is something more,
Hoping you're doing the right thing.

Wondering what your children will remember about this time,
Worrying about doing the right thing,
Hoping everyone will be just fine.

Hoping things get better soon.

Whatever you're wondering,
worrying about,
hoping for...

Remember, you are not alone.

19th April, 2020

## The Baby Shower that didn't happen

To our wonderful friend Alicia,
On your baby shower day,
We're gutted we can't be there,
But this is what we want to say.

You have waited so long for this time,
And we couldn't be happier for you,
We can't wait to see your new baby in your arms,
And your lovely floral top covered in poo!

We can't wait to see Nancy,
Give her new love a warm embrace,
We can't wait to see Gary,
Look so proud on his beaming face.

When these crazy times are over,
We hope to see you as soon as we can,
We might even come for a peek through the window,
Because of the visiting ban.

Embrace the new smells,
Enjoy the sleepless nights,
Enjoy everything that makes this feel so right.
You deserve it.

We just have one request to ask,
Please don't go over the top,
When you're finally choosing that special name,
Don't call it Jurgen or Klopp!


20th April, 2020

## **Alternative Nursery Rhymes for 2020: Part One**

This little piggy stayed at home,
This little piggy stayed at home,
This little piggy had roast beef,
And this little piggy had none.
And this little piggy went all the way to Tesco and came back
without any flour.

Jack and Jill went up the hill,
But only for an hour a day,
Jack fell down and washed his hands,
And Jill came tumbling after, two metres behind due to social
distancing laws.

The grand old Duke of York,
He had ten thousand men,
He marched them up to the top of the hill,
Then made them socially isolate for 12 weeks.

Twinkle Twinkle little star,
How have I never realised how beautiful you are?
Up above the world so high,
Like a diamond in the sky,
Twinkle Twinkle little star,
I will never ignore how wonderful you are.

If you're happy and you know it clap your hands,
If you're happy and you know it clap your hands,
If you're happy and you know it and you really want to show it,
Then stand on your doorstep every Thursday and clap for the
NHS.

21st April, 2020

## Alternative Nursery Rhymes for 2020: Part Two

Row, row, row your boat,
Gently down the stream,
You've made in your living room,
From cushions, a blue blanket and some cardboard boxes.

Humpty Dumpty sat on a wall,
Humpty Dumpty had a great cough,
All the NHS doctors and nurses put him back together again,
Because that's just what they do.

The wheels on the bus go round and round,
Round and round, round and round,
The wheels on the bus go round and round,
Taking key workers to work in the deserted towns.

Mary had a little lamb,
Its fleece was white as snow,
And everywhere that Mary didn't go,
The lamb didn't go either.

Polly put the kettle on,
Polly put the kettle on,
Polly put the kettle on,
Fifteen times a day.

22nd April, 2020

## April 23rd, St. George's Day

A dragon was slain by our patron saint George it would seem,
What a shame he's not still alive today,
To pierce the heart of this beast named Covid-19.
It might not breathe fire,
But it's burning a hole in our society.

Of one thing I can be certain,
We won't wave a white flag in the face of this monster.
We'll keep staying at home,
We'll keep washing our hands,
We'll keep on fighting.

Saints in the 21st century wear a different kind of armour
(if they can get it)
They call it PPE.
Masks, scrubs and plastic gloves,
Determined to destroy the enemy.
With shields ready to defend,
They wait for the order to attack.

Of one thing I can be certain,
We won't wave a white flag in the face of this monster.
We'll keep staying at home,
We'll keep washing our hands,
We'll keep clapping for the NHS.

23rd April, 2020

## Is the curve flattening?

Is the *curve* flattening?
Have we reached the *peak*?
It's all we seek to discover,
As we *socially distance* week by week.

Words such as *plateau* and the *reproduction number* R,
Verbs commanding us to *save, protect* and *stay*.
All these words repeated over and over again,
As we listen intently to what the experts say.

In the meantime, at home,
The words we hear the most,
Are not as scientific,
*Tea, bake, quiz, zoom* and *post*!

Of all these words we're hearing every day,
The word *vaccine* brings some hope,
The first volunteers were injected
yesterday,
It's now the scientists from Oxford who are under the
microscope.

So whatever words you use today,
If it's a good day or if you're feeling blue,
Just think how we are creating history now,
And we're all part of it together, me and you.


24th April, 2020

## Max and his tea bag

From his garden in Morecambe to a tea bag factory,
To the USA where he was helped by 'Back to the Future' star
Marty,
To his friend Osh in Wales and his auntie in France,
Max is conquering the world, taking his chance.

His teabag of choice is definitely Typhoo,
If you get in touch he can throw it to you!
His little bag of tea has flown over 50,000 miles.
And with it it's bringing so many smiles.

What a great idea of Max and his tea-loving family,
He's proved homework can be fun with some creativity,
When someone asks Max what he's done the last few days,
He can ask his Typhoo teabag friend and see what he says!


25th April, 2020

## London without the Marathon

Today the streets of London should be overflowing with runners,
In their trusty trainers
Trained and timed to perfection.
Their unique number pinned to their vest.
A badge of honour.

Today the streets of London should be overwhelmed with
emotional
spectators,
Charity campaigners,
Medics, volunteers,
All kinds of supporters.
Brass bands competing with the voices of local radio.

Instead, all will be silent.

I don't know about you,
But it's the music that gets me every time.
'The Trap' by Ron Goodwin I believe,
It always sends a tingle down my spine.

Because on this day I'm always reminded of a special time,
The day my dad ran the marathon 26.2 miles.
On the banks of The Thames mum and I stood,
Staring at the tsunami of runners,
Pouring into the streets.

We waited for that moment, that few seconds in time,
When he ran past us, giving us the thumbs up sign.
The tin foil cape he was given at the end made him look strange:
A sweating chocolate bar!
(the race was sponsored by Mars back then).

It's a parent's job to be proud of their children,
But on this day, I was proud of my dad.
He gave me a memory I will never forget.
I'm telling him now; I don't think I've told him yet!

Today should have been the biggest single fundraising day in
Britain.
A huge hole that will hopefully be filled,
On the 4th October,
When, fingers and feet crossed,
Those trusty trainers will be put back on,
And the crowds will once again throng the streets of London.

26th April, 2020

## A stroll on the canal

A stroll on the canal
Offers an abundance of wildlife.
All for free.
All au-naturel.
Nothing fake or false.

A paddling of ducklings follow in their parents' slipstream,
They are nurtured and encouraged to survive on their own,
They are loved and love unconditionally.

Cherry blossom confetti celebrates the many unions of nature,
Colourful carnivals and ceremonies take place in all habitats,
No matter what species,
No matter which gender,
No matter what colour.

No stone is the same;
some rough and weathered,
some perfectly smooth,
They are not judged on their appearance,
They are not ostracised because they are different.

The downy head of the dandelion clock,
So fragile and delicate,
Is easily wounded,
A bit like our feelings.

The trickle of a stream runs freely,
Pebbles splash and plonk when they hit the water,
They may sink,
But they never give up.

A fallen leaf feels neglected and ignored,
Lonely and unappreciated,
But there is always a hand there,
To reach out and pick it up.

Birds compete during the dawn chorus,
Each has its own unique call,
Each has its repertoire of songs,
They don't try to silence the voices of others.

I guess we can all learn something from nature.


27th April, 2020

## Lockdown in the living room

The living room/front room/lounge:
A place to relax and unwind,
A place of sanctuary after a busy day at work,
Now it seems its purpose is a very different kind.

A classroom,
A workplace,
An office,
A crèche.
A place where there always seems to be loads of mess!

A meeting place (virtually of course),
An art studio,
A hairdressers,
A den.
When it will return to normal, we don't know when.

A dance studio,
A picnic site,
A recording studio,
A park.
The only time it's remotely tidy seems to be after dark.

A football stadium,
A gymnasium,
A place of adventure and fun,
A cafe, restaurant and bar,
All rolled into one.

I guess it can be anything,
If you use your imagination.
Thank goodness no one will see the mess,
For as long as we're in isolation.

28th April, 2020

## Just Dance!

Calling all you TikTok dancers!
Today is International Dance Day,
So if you're planning a new routine,
Then why not perform it today!

It's a worldwide event that celebrates all genres of dance,
Whether it's those who are talented or those who simply prance,
Those who pretend by shuffling side to side,
Or those who have perfected the waltz's glide.

Those who like the intensity of the tango,
Or the fabulous frivolous fandango,
Those who appreciate the art of street,
Even those who cannot dance because they have two left feet!

From the pirouettes, pliés and passé of ballet,
To those who perform the sashay,
To the funky flash-mobbers and the disco queens,
Who know all the moves to those to annoying routines.

Those who learn to dance in the name of romance,
A raunchy rumba or rehearsed first wedding dance,
Flamenco, foxtrot or a bit of northern soul,
To those who use their belly or even a pole!

If you shimmy to the samba or the sensational salsa,
Prefer rock and roll or the cha cha cha,
Go on, just have a go, it'll make you feel alive,
Grab someone close to you and have a little jive!

So, why not have a dance in the supermarket queue,
To celebrate this festival of dance,
Or bust a few moves as you do your daily walk,
If it doesn't make people laugh, it's sure to make them talk.

29th April, 2020

## Two Men United During Lockdown

I hope many positive things will come out of this difficult time,
One thing I hope is that we will all be more kind.
I was so touched by this story of kindness yesterday,
I decided to make it my verse's focus for today.

A homeless man named Chris has been staying in a hotel,
After the owner offered to rescue him from hell,
Chris has been living in luxury and eating like a king,
He's been treated with respect, not disregarded as a 'thing'.

Before the pandemic Mike didn't help the homeless on the street,
Those who sat in doorways and begged at his feet,
He'd walk past them like most of us do,
Not really understanding the person, the how and the who.

The hotel boss, Mike, treats Chris like a guest,
He's had a massive impact on this man who was depressed,
He's taken him under his protective 4 star wing,
He's listened and is still listening,   without judging.

Breaking down barriers is what's happening here,
Chris is a changed man, that is very clear,
Mike regards his new guests as his extended family,
He has offered them friendship and has saved their sanity.

I know there's many hoteliers who are doing just this,
But when we clap tonight I'll be thinking of Mike and Chris,
Prejudices from both of them have been put to one side,
And they are both reaping the rewards of just being kind.

30th April, 2020

## Firefighters Clap Too!

So there we were getting ready to clap,
I'd changed out of my joggers and put on some slap,
Sprayed a bit of hairspray to tame my wild hair,
And attempted to cover the grey hairs lurking there.

When all of a sudden a fire engine drove past,
As you can imagine, our doors opened pretty fast,
The threat of rain and the ominous clouds,
Couldn't stop us cheering extra loud.

Blue lights flashing and sirens switched on,
It was the best Thursday night out bar none,
What a lovely gesture of the firefighters to lead the applause,
To recognise their fellow emergency workers who are committed
to the cause.

So thanks Lancashire Fire Service,
You really made our night,
It was great to see your smiling faces,
As the country continues to fight.

1st May, 2020

## The Flour Shortage

The shortage of flour,
Is preventing people baking,
Whether it's bread, biscuits or buns,
Their knead is real!

The problem is nothing to do with quantity,
It's more to do with how it's packed,
There's not enough flour packers to go round,
The flour packers are not getting though the stack.

I blame Paul Hollywood.
He might have lovely eyes and be a bit of a stud,
But he's got a lot to answer for,
Encouraging us to make our own pies and puds.

Mary Berry's also to blame,
Her bottom's never been a soggy one,
She always makes the perfect sponge,
Or a fantastic, fluffy, fruit scone.

To all you bored bakers out there,
Whether you're a newbie or a pro,
Hope you acquire some flour soon,
In the meantime, why not sew?

2nd May, 2020

## The Doll's House

I've often wondered what it would be like to live inside a doll's
house,
To be something miniature, even smaller than a harvest mouse,
To live there rent or mortgage free,
Where everywhere is always clean and tidy.

Inside the doll's house we think everything is safe and bright,
No one to judge, everything just right,
No ants crawling out of crevices you didn't know existed,
No one trying to catch you out, no words twisted.

That's not to say that dolls in doll's houses are happy all the time,
I imagine it can be quite lonely and miserable sometimes,
Not having the freedom to come and go as you choose,
Having someone watching you and controlling your every move.

Doll's houses like these exist everywhere.
We walk past them and don't see the despair.
We can't possibly understand even if we tried,
The hell some men and women experience, with no place to hide.

3rd May, 2020

*This poem was inspired by a person who phoned into a very popular daytime show
last week and told just a small part of their story. And by the shocking data from
the charity Refuge that says calls to its helpline have risen 49% to 400 a day
during lockdown.*

## May the fourth be with you

May the fourth be with you,
You Star Wars fans,
I don't share your passion,
And I really don't understand,
The strength of feeling you have for George Lucas' creation,
But I wish you a happy day as you celebrate across the nation.


May the fourth, 2020

## The Soundtrack of Lockdown

It's difficult to describe the soundtrack of lockdown,
It can't really be downloaded, saved or shared.
But it would definitely be a massive hit
On the radio, if ever it was aired.

I'm talking about the soundtrack of nature.
The streets are sleeping but the birds are awake,
In full voice
In gardens,
Along canals,
Surrounding lakes,
In woodlands,
On pavements next to the quiet roads,
My mum said she could hear it when we were talking on the
phone.

They have less competition I guess,
They're not overpowered by aggressive HGVs
Or screaming school children waiting for the bus
Or robotic commuters, always in a rush.

A reporter on the news asked a little girl,
'How do you feel when you hear the birds sing?'
'Happy' was her one word reply.
Her whole face was smiling.

Bucolic bliss.
Birdsong.
The soundtrack of lockdown.
Free to anyone who stops...
And listens.

5th May, 2020

## In six months' time…

Christmas will be a few weeks away.
For too many families it will be their first without a precious loved one,
The first of many where an empty chair sits at the table,
The first of many where brave faces are put on,
Where tears are lovingly wiped away by a compassionate hand.

For too many families it will be the hardest time of all,
The uncertainty about the future.
Parents working all the extra hours they can,
Trying to make up for lost time and earnings.

In six months' time…
I wonder if we'll still hear about trolley rage in supermarkets?
If we'll now stock pile sprouts instead?
If we'll order online delivery then complain
When get we get self-raising flour instead of bread?

Will we still give to charity like we usually do?
Will we still donate to food banks and charity shops?
Will we still think of others, me and you?
When the Thursday night clapping stops?

Do we really need to worry how we will look in our Christmas party dress?
Will we still spend a fortune on beauty treatments we don't need?
Will be still worry about the silly things which cause us so much stress?
Will we still buy too many things to satisfy our greed?

In six months' time…
I hope we'll still be clapping,
Singing, hugging, kissing and dancing too.
Spreading happiness, compassion and love, not germs,
I hope for all of this, what about you?

6th May, 2020

## 50 poems written

Tomorrow I'm celebrating my 50th.
Half a century.
The big five 0
No, not a special birthday!
But poems.
50 of them!

When I wrote my first poem on 20th March,
School had just closed.
The students had left my classroom then I came home too.
Lockdown was about to start.
We had no idea what was in store,
How many lives would be torn apart.

Little did I know how much writing poems would help me,
It's actually been like some sort of therapy,
Helping me through the good days and the bad,
Giving me a purpose when I've felt sad.

Thanks to everyone who has commented, shared and liked,
I'm chuffed at how people have responded to the words I've typed,
I'll keep on writing, for how long I really can't say,
And maybe I'll get lucky and someone will publish them one day.

7th May, 2020

## **VE Day 75 years**

Bunting and flags dominate our view,
As we look out of our kitchen window.
Different shades of red, white and blue,
Pictures of poppies, soldiers and rainbows too.

We're ready and waiting to pay our respects,
We'll be commemorating from our gardens and doorsteps.
We'll celebrate and cheer after the serene silence at eleven,
Remembering those still with us now and those looking down
from heaven.

We'll be singing along later tonight,
As Dame Vera's voice leads the way.
She's performed in Egypt, India and Burma.
But she'll be here on our street singing with us today.

It's ironic that we're thinking about freedom when we're not
allowed much at all,
But today's not about us, instead a poignant celebration,
It's about the heroes, their bravery and their sacrifice
As they fought for our freedom and to protect our nation

VE
Victorious. Exceptional.
Valiant. Extraordinary.

VE Day 75.
May 8th, 2020.
We will meet again.

8th May, 2020

## Our First Night Out in a While

It's Billy Joel's birthday today,
When I was a little girl I had his album on cassette.
Danced side to side to *Uptown Girl,*
Those memories I'll never forget.

*Scenes from an Italian restaurant* and *Piano Man,*
We saw him see him perform live in 2018,
Our first night out together since Isla was born,
It was one of the best shows I've ever seen.

He really is a legend is Billy,
*My Life* and *Longest Time* are two of my faves,
A voice that sings with emotion and grit,
Thanks Billy, for those memories you gave.

So, this morning we'll listen to a bit of Spotify,
And imagine we're back there that sunny night,
Where his powerful, booming voice,
Made everything feel just right.


9th May, 2020

## Quizzing

I wonder if the lockdown
Will improve the nation's average IQ?
My general knowledge is definitely being tested,
With the number of quizzes we do.

It's something we look forward to,
I know it sounds a bit sad.
But we haven't got much to talk about
So when it's quiz night, we're glad.

My knowledge of American states
Has definitely improved,
But I'm not sure how that will help me
When the lockdown's removed.

We've also been watching episodes of Tenable and The Chase,
There are some strange questions on there.
Yesterday was 10 ingredients in Allinson's seeds and grain bread
Followed by the first 10 four letter words of Bon Jovi's *Livin' on a Prayer!*

If virtual quizzing is keeping your brain ticking over,
And helping to keep you sane,
Hope you're learning some wonderful facts,
To use when the actual pub quiz starts up again.

10th May, 2020

## A New Arrival during Lockdown

Through the window greetings,
FaceTime first meetings,
Brief but precious sightings,
The little wave was worth waiting for.

Inside the beautiful woollen blanket
Nests a bundle of hope,
Uttering the most delicate squirmy sounds,
A fluffy downy duckling.
A symbol of innocence,
Not a care in the world.

Tiny pink fingers,
Grip so tightly,
A little hold of your hand,
Means so much more
Than they'll ever understand.

Birth in lockdown is not how we want it to be,
Because the family visits can't happen as planned,
But do not doubt for one minute,
The care of the midwives there on hand.

More importantly, nothing can take away,
The overwhelming feeling of pride and joy,
Which gives us all a lovely feeling inside,
When this uncertain world welcomes a new little girl or boy.

11th May, 2020

## Hair Issues

According to research I read, human hair grows 6 inches per year,
Mine is definitely bucking the trend.
I wonder if there will still be demand for hair extensions,
When this lockdown comes to an end?

Foods that help your hair to grow,
Are avocado, eggs, spinach and fish,
So if you want locks to rival Rapunzel by the start of July,
I'd go for a protein-rich dish.

But if you're considering using the kitchen scissors,
To give your hair a quick little trim,
I'd think again if I were you,
The chances of a positive result are unfortunately pretty slim.

Wait for the expert to get their skilled hands on your hair,
But be prepared to fight for an appointment when they finally re-
open their chair!

12th May, 2020

## A Disease of the Mind

A vile vicious tweet,
I saw on Twitter the other night,
Containing details of racist remarks,
Sent to footballer Ian Wright.

No matter where your footballing allegiance lies,
Whose kit you wear, whose autograph has been signed,
Which team you support, whose autobiographies you buy,
Surely we must always respect and always be kind.

In a time when we should all be supporting each other,
Thinking with our heads and our hearts,
The last thing society needs,
Is people ripping each other apart.

'I'm normally better at ignoring it'
Was Ian Wright's reaction,
But it shouldn't be ignored, should it?
It needs firm and decisive action.

A few weeks ago on a Match of the Day special,
Wright talked about the prejudice he has had to endure,
And how hard it has been as a professional player,
It will be with him forever, I'm sure.

So, why I am writing this?
Because it really makes me so sad,
Because he's not only been a footballer,
He's a son, a husband, a dad.

We've said it before but we'll say it again,
Kick it out, respect, be kind,
How many slogans do we need?
Until we defeat this dreadful disease of the mind?

13th May, 2020

## **What about the Grandparents?**

Golfers are returning to the fairways,
Putting and chipping once more.
Gardeners are tending their greens,
With plants they've bought from the store.

But grandparents are still in the bunkers,
Grandad is still in the rough,
Grandma is out of bounds,
And they are finding it all so tough.


14th May, 2020

## <u>Why Eurovision means so much to me</u>

It was supposed to be Eurovision this weekend,
It's always had a place in my heart.
It's when Paul and I first got together,
In our history, this was the start.

The host and winning country was Greece,
It was May 2005.
We were all told to wear fancy dress,
But, wrapped in a Swedish flag, he walked down the drive!

The winning song was called 'My Number One',
I don't recall if it was a memorable tune.
But I guess that title was quite apt,
As we kissed under the light of the moon.

But don't worry I'm not going to get soppy,
Or write ridiculously romantic rhymes,
But that's why Eurovision is more than a song contest to me,
It marks the beginning of my time with this husband of mine.

15th May, 2020

## <u>Driving in Lockdown</u>

I went out in the car yesterday,
For the first time in weeks,
It felt very strange.

Instead of birdsong, the radio blared out
Lady Gaga's 'Poker Face',
Different to the chatter and cheep of the sparrow.

I felt like I'd just passed my test.
A bit like one of the ducklings on the canal,
I took extra care, taking in my surroundings.

The world still does exist,
Beyond our house, garden and street,
But if felt good to be home.
Back to our sanctuary.
Our own little safe retreat.


16th May, 2020

### A Walk in the Woods

A carpet of wild garlic invited us into the woods,
A sensory delight.
Tiny white delicate flowers with a strong scent,
Demanded our attention.

The bark of faceless decayed tree trunks,
Snapped and cracked,
As the cows in the adjoining field
Watched
And stared.

Climbing over the stile,
And watching our footing,
We made our way to the clearing,
Ate Jammie Dodgers and shared some orange squash.
And took in the view,
The open, green and blue view.

And we just breathed.
Just listened.
Just whispered.
Respecting the noise of nature.
Thankful to live where we live.

17th May, 2020

## The Animals are Taking Over

The animals are taking over,
The animals are moving in,
Taking over the spaces,
We normally reserve for ourselves.

Kangaroos are window-shopping in Adelaide,
Sheep are spinning on roundabouts in Wales,
Deer are dozing in England's parks.

Ducks are promenading down streets in Paris,
Lions are testing out their hole-in-one ability on golf courses in
South Africa,
Bears are out for their afternoon stroll in California.

Birds are flocking to the beach in Peru,
Elephants are out for an early morning stroll in India,
Pigs are using zebra crossings to escort their families across roads.

I'm actually quite envious,
Of them being allowed to roam,
Enjoying their freedom,
In the places we call home.

19th May, 2020

## The Coronacoaster

We're all feeling the ups and downs
during this pandemic disease,
One minute we're loving lockdown, thinking this whole thing is a
breeze.

Making the most of the opportunities we've got,
Thinking positive, no matter what.

Always looking on the bright side,
Trying to take everything in our stride.

The next minute we feel anxious and begin to get weepy,
Exhausted, fed up and just so sleepy.

Feeling flat and lacking any get-up-and-go,
Worrying about things makes us feel so low.

Going for a walk sounds like too much hard work,
In the mind, negative thoughts start to lurk.

That's the coronacoaster.
The clouds and the rain make us blue,
But as the sunshine returns,
The positive feelings will too.

There's nothing wrong with admitting,
This whole thing is getting us down,
But as long as we keep talking we'll be okay,
And slowly the smiles will replace our frowns.

20th May, 2020

## Nature Morte

I don't know about you,
But I don't usually win the raffle,
Maybe an occasional bottle of wine or box of chocs,
But it's not often my ticket is picked out of the box.

I read about a lady from Italy,
Who won one of Picasso's works of art,
A painting in oil from 1921,
A still life. Nature Morte.

The painting is of a glass of absinthe and a newspaper,
I wonder what was going through his head when he created this,
Is there a hidden message,
Something we could easily miss?

Avoid newspapers but drink alcohol?
Avoid alcohol and read newspapers?
Do both at once?
Never touch either?

Whatever the message,
One thing is true,
I'm steering clear of newspapers,
Like any teacher should do.

The headlines are always disparaging,
Criticising everything we do,
We're not heroes, we don't want to be,
We're just used to being shamed by those who haven't a clue.

Anyway, back to the raffle and this lady's prize,
It's worth a million euros they say.
What an absolute treat for her in these times,
Just think of all those lazy teachers she could pay!

21st May, 2020

## 'While there is tea, there is hope.' (Arthur Wing Pinero)

In unsettling times,
A cup of tea makes everything better.
Which is why the tea company PG,
Has written their rivals a letter.

PG are proposing a National Tea Break slot,
No matter what your choice of tea,
They want us to stop what we're doing and have a cuppa,
Every afternoon at three.

So, just before 3pm today put the kettle on,
Grab your cup and make yourself a brew.
Have a chat and check in with someone you know,
Maybe treat yourself to a biscuit too!

Whilst there is tea, there is hope.
Whilst there is hope, there is tea.

22nd May, 2020

## Real Faces

I've seen some lovely human faces,
In real life (not online) this week,
All socially distanced of course,
But it's felt like such a treat!

I've seen real life friends on their doorsteps or when walking on
the prom,
I've enjoyed chatting with them, having a real life talk.
Their hair slightly longer, but styled with aplomb.
Their faces freckled and sun-kissed from all the sunny lockdown
walks.

I've seen real life colleagues not phone numbers and email
addresses,
We've shared our lockdown highs and lows and some of our
stresses,
It's been so nice to see people even from afar,
Sometimes having a chat with the window down in the car.

What struck me most,
Was that I could actually see their eyes!
Eyes that may have shed the occasional lockdown tear,
But, like their laughs and smiles, seem to hide or mask their fears.

I've enjoyed the adult conversation,
Even though it's been very brief,
Makes a change from Ben and Holly, Peppa Pig and Bing,
I've been able to talk normally rather than feeling like I have to
sing.

I've missed the face-to-face contact,
The eye to eye contact too,
Hopefully it won't be that long,
Until we can see our loved ones in real life too.

23rd May, 2020

## **Practise what you preach**

So we are being told to
Stay alert,
Control the virus,
Save lives.

In return I'd like to say...

Learn how to use the apostrophe,
It won't save us from this catastrophe,
But it might make you look less foolish.

Practise what you preach,
That means no trips to the beach,
Or Barnard Castle.

Save lives,
Avoid long distance drives,
Especially to elderly parents.

Start to be alert like we are,
Start to help us control the virus,
Start to help us to try to save lives.

24th May, 2020

## Spring Bank Holiday

May Spring Bank Holiday in lockdown,
Kind of feels upside down,
Inside out,
Back to front,
Strange.

No day trips to the Lakes,
No lunch at the pub,
No weekend mini breaks,
No motorway queues,
No meeting up with friends,
No ice cream in the park,
But we'll still make the most,
Of the day until it's dark.

One May tradition will suffer this year,
Cheese-rolling in Gloucestershire,
No one will win a wheel of Double Gloucester,
For tumbling head-over-heels like an out of control tyre.

Talking of cheese, I stay loyal to home with my choice,
Wensleydale or Lancashire are my top two,
And even though it's a bit pongy,
I love a bit of Garstang Blue.

Anyway, have a Happy Bank Holiday Monday,
Whatever you decide to arrange,
Try to make it different from the other eight Mondays we've had,
Since our world became very strange.


25th May, 2020

## The Padlocked Playgrounds

Walking past the padlocked public playgrounds,
Where the sad and lonely swings and slides reside,
One can't help but notice,
How overgrown the grass has become inside.

Proud armies of dandelion clocks try to command the sprawling weeds,
Occupying this deserted land, they've taken over, they're in control,
As our confused children look on and await their turn so patiently,
In the parks there's no laughter, no fun, no soul.

This has to be the longest queue for the swings to date,
But at least we all know this land will be ours once again.
Whereas the dandelions and other weeds can't escape their fate,
When the council mowers defeat the enemy, our children's territory we will regain.

26th May, 2020

## **One Tuesday early evening during Lockdown**

Friesian cows crossed the road in front of our car,
A farmer on a quad bike trailing behind them, encouraging them
to walk.
Taking their time, they gave us chance to admire their black and
white markings,
Almost like they were models on a catwalk.

Then later, the cows seemed to be walking alongside us,
As if they were escorting us off their patch,
We'd stuffed our faces with fish and chips and cans of fizzy pop,
Before having a little football match.

All socially distanced of course.
Us that is, not the cows.

Tuesday early evening during lockdown ain't so bad.

27th May, 2020

## Gardening

When lockdown first started,
Isla and I planted some seeds,
Now parsley, basil and micro cress.
Have grown, minus the weeds.

I'm not quite sure how the carrots will turn out,
But whatever the outcome, we've enjoyed watching them grow,
I was given a tomato plant last week,
Now we're waiting for the tiny fruits to say hello.

The scent of sweet peas is starting to linger on the breeze,
There's no flowers just yet, but they're starting to tease,
These delicate flowers remind me of my grandad,
That I've inherited his love of gardening, I think he'd be quite glad.

Isla seems to have green fingers too,
She helps by giving the plants some water,
Gardening has become something more special now,
Because it's something I do with my daughter.

28th May, 2020

## The Last Night we Clapped

Last night we clapped for the final time,
To thank all those who are keeping Britain going,
Who still risk their lives every single day,
In such tough conditions for inadequate pay.

Although the clapping has come to an end,
The gratitude will always prevail,
I don't think we'll ever forget our Thursday nights,
Our appreciation for those who help us fight.

Society's love for the NHS must keep growing,
So they FINALLY get the respect owing.

It's now about their mental health and support,
Recovery of a different sort,
Because their eyes will never unsee,
Their ears will never unhear,
Their hearts will never stop breaking,
Their minds will never forget,
The experiences. The deaths.
The leftovers of this killer disease
Will never disappear.

29th May, 2020

## To Gather Together

I can't wait to see friends and family,
To gather together at last,
But I can't help thinking,
That all this is going way too fast.

I don't mean to be a party pooper,
And I don't want to be downcast,
I just hope that this period of sunshine,
Doesn't end with a depressing forecast.


30th May, 2020

## Just the Three of Us

Two lines.
One blue,
One golden brown,
Sky and sand united.
A never-ending togetherness.
Peace and tranquility.
Our escape. Our sanctuary.

If that lovely couple of hours,
End up being our little beach holiday this year,
Then, we will be happy.
Sandcastles, sandy shoes and sand in our sandwiches.
Just the three of us.
Perfect.

31st May, 2020

## Drive-thru Ice Cream

Drive-thru ice cream,
It was definitely worth the time it took to queue,
Jaffa cake, rainbow and strawberry dream,
Fantastic flavours, to name but a few.

It's actually proving quite easy,
To support local shops and spend,
When the quality is tip-top, first-rate,
We've pledged to continue this when lockdown ends.

We'd much rather give our money to our community,
Than feed the greedy superstores,
Village traders need our business and our loyalty,
But over the coming months they'll need our cash even more.

1st June, 2020

## <u>Covidiots</u>

I can understand people getting up at the crack of dawn,
To go for a walk or a run,
To take in the views,
To listen to the birds
And bask in the morning sun,

To enjoy the countryside or town in peace,
To make the most of the day,
I imagine it is quite beautiful,
A sense of well-being
A kind of release.

But getting up early to queue outside IKEA.
At 5.40 am.
In the sun.
For hours.
The word 'covidiot' springs to mind.

No wonderful views,
Just the back of someone's head,
The smell of petrol fumes,
And the burning of sensitive skin as it starts to turn red.

No matter how desperate I am for a new mattress for the bed,
Or a new floral vase,
There's no way I'd contemplate that,
I'd rather sleep outside under the stars.

2nd June, 2020

## Where do kisses come from?

Where do kisses come from?
Isla asked me yesterday,
What a brilliant question,
I didn't know what to say!

Where do kisses come from?
Where do I start?
Kisses come from the heart,
From those who feel love,
From those who are no longer with us,
Who watch us from above.

Kisses come from inside your head,
They come through your lips and make a funny sound,
You always have kisses before you go to bed,
They accompany a cuddle when you wrap your arms around.

You can blow people kisses if you can't see them face-to-face,
But a kiss on the cheek, you can never replace.

Am loving her questions, her inquisitive mind,
Why do we wee on the toilet?
What does a butterfly eat?
So many questions of different kinds,
So many questions, the answers she will find.


3rd June, 2020

## Socially distanced schooling

Socially distanced schooling,
Doesn't feel like schooling at all,
From a distance means,
There's a barrier, a bit like a wall.

No subtle whispers of encouragement,
No quiet supportive phrase,
No close-up coaxing or cajoling,
Or hushed words of praise.

No offering a helping hand,
Or a shoulder on which to cry,
Just clear boundaries about boundaries,
And we all know the reasons why.

But it's what we have to do,
We have to change our ways,
So that we do the best that we can,
In the coming months, weeks and days.

All the natural things we do,
Like walking from desk to desk,
Looking over shoulders to check, point out, correct,
We can no longer do which will feel very strange,
Everything now should be safe, from a 2 metre range.

But we CAN use our voices,
To welcome, reassure and praise,
We CAN read and share and sing,
And question in many different ways.

We CAN use our ears to listen to what our students say,
We CAN answer their questions and try to help them on their
way,
We CAN use our eyes to give them 'that look',
We CAN tell if they're feeling down,

We CAN use our washed hands to applaud their hard work,
We CAN make smiles from frowns.


Socially distanced schooling,
Doesn't feel like schooling at all,
But the most important thing in all of this,
It's that we'll be there to help them climb over that wall.


4th June, 2020

## Thursday nights are not the same

Thursday nights are different now,
They used to be the highlight of our week,
Instead we're all behind closed doors,
All praying that there won't be a second peak.

We missed going out to clap last night,
But still hope the NHS staff get the recognition they deserve.
No clapping doesn't mean our gratitude stops,
We hope they know they're respected by us, those they serve.


5th June, 2020

## The Tip

I've made an appointment
To go to the tip.

Let me say that again...
I've made an appointment
To go to the tip.

Not the dentists,
Or the beauty salon,
Or the hairdressers.

The tip.

To get rid of more tat,
Stuff we've seemed to hoard,
One positive of living in lockdown,
There's no time to be bored.

The last time we tidied the garage I was pregnant, had a massive
bump,
We found a dead dried-up frog that day,
An early labour nearly came on when I saw the dreadful sight,
I wonder what treasure we will discover today?

6th June, 2020

## Blowing the Cobwebs Away

Balancing carefully like acrobats on a circus high-wire,
We walked over the uneven beach rocks and pebbles,
No two the same shape, some perfectly smooth.
It was precarious underfoot,
Especially for little feet,
But we blew the cobwebs away.

The phrase 'blowing the cobwebs away'
Originated in the 18th century,
The name given to cleaning the cobwebs from one's house,
But now means the clearing of heads whilst out on a brisk walk.
Clearing our heads was needed with all this 'R' talk.

There was nothing brisk about our walk on the shore yesterday,
Not with little feet in tow,
But the gusty wind certainly blew any cobwebs away,
And made the three of us aglow,
As we watched the seawater come and go.


7th June, 2020

## A Weekend of Ups and Downs

Cancelled holiday flights,
Awaiting refunds for activities we can no longer do,
Their planes and our plans on hold.

Questioning of quarantine rules,
The aggressive sights and sounds and protests,
Wear masks we're now being told.

Football in nanna and grandad's peaceful garden,
Eating ice cream and chocolate treats,
Making memories like this are worth much more than gold.

Walks to see the swans and their cygnets,
Each determined to survive,
Nature teaches her lessons, to be brave and bold.

The ups and downs of this weekend,
Are something on which we will always reflect,
Whether we're young or whether we're old.

8th June, 2020

## Ferroequinologists

Trainspotting.
The hobby. Not the film.
I've never understood it.
Never really 'got' it.

The closest we get is Thomas the Tank on the telly,
And Isla gets excited when we see a train,
The compulsory 'choo choo' resounds as it passes us by,
She asks if it's daddy's train and, if not, why?

Stood on the railway bridge by the shore,
Enthusiasts waited, wanting more.
Their phones out ready to capture the moment...

I expected a magnificent engine,
A steam locomotive.
The Flying Scotsman.

But no...
A diesel guzzling monster,
Followed by an army of freight containers,
Hurtled past at speed.
I guess that's the appeal for a ferroequinologist.
Now, there's a good word for Tuesday morning.


9th June, 2020

## Carpe Diem

The fact we can't plan anything,
Is not good for those with OCD,
Those who like to be in control,
Those people just like me.

But this whole experience,
Is helping me to overcome this,
We can't plan anything,
And when we do make plans, they go amiss.

A phrase used by Roman poet Horace,
Springs to mind at this time,
One should enjoy life while one can,
Carpe diem is the message of this rhyme.

Live for the moment.
Seize the day.
Carpe diem.
In the rain today.

10th June, 2020

## Ambulance

If you ever need a reminder of how amazing the NHS is,
The documentary 'Ambulance' is well worth a watch,
The care and love those people give,
They don't just save lives, they WILL people to live.

It takes a very special person to do that job,
Of that there can be no doubt,
Facing death in the face every day,
Always being there, come what may.

Dealing with those who lose someone close,
Being a shoulder to cry on, when someone needs it the most,
I do nothing but cry when I watch it on TV,
And think what safe hands I'd be in if they were sent to look after me.

They say they're just doing their job,
But to me it's far more than that,
The compassion and patience those paramedics show,
Is more valued than they'll ever know.

11<sup>th</sup> June, 2020

## **One Day**

Perspex screens,
Barriers and coloured tape,
Circles with feet on the floor.

Lines, arrows and one way routes,
Down aisles, in factories, in schools,
Sanitiser and spray by the door.

Whether it's offices, schools or shops,
Post offices, takeaways or banks,
Things don't feel the same anymore.

Maybe one day these screens, sneeze guards and signs,
Will be a thing of the past,
And we'll have won this battle,
One day. At last.


12th June, 2020

## Car, Car, Truck, Jeep

Whilst queuing to get into a high street shop yesterday,
'Not just any' high street shop,
You know the one I mean,
The name I don't need to say.

Isla decided she wanted to sing,
So started with the opening line of her favourite song,
'Car, Car, Truck, Jeep'
(you sing to the tune of Baa Baa Black Sheep).

At first no one seemed to notice,
As she sang the words I know so well,
But after a while others started to smile,
They were impressed, I could tell!

I don't think they'd heard the words before,
About the digger and dumper truck,
But we've learnt it off by heart,
It's two years since we got the book.

As I was deciding what to buy for tea,
A lady stopped and spoke to us,
And said what a lovely little song,
About the aeroplane and the bus.

She said Isla had brought some
Positivity to people in the queue,
And how people were smiling because of her rhyme,
How people felt better after hearing Isla sing,
I'm considering charging a small fee when she sings the next time!

13th June, 2020

## Canal Boat Dreaming

I've always romanticised about having a canal boat,
I think it stems from our old trips with Strivs, our Captain John,
So many memories of special days out,
Days that now seem long gone.

The sense of freedom on one of those boats,
Just feels so alluring, especially now,
Being able to stop wherever you choose,
Kind of like your being on your own mini cruise.

Don't get me wrong I know at times it must be hard,
There must always be a job to do,
Having to maintain, clean and paint the boat,
Whilst moored up at the boat yard.

But the independence and joy that I guess must be felt,
The peace and the calm of the natural noise,
Just the birds, ducks and swans for company,
How wonderful it must be...

I thought about all of this as we strolled near Tewitfield Locks,
Canal surrounded by endless fields of green,
And once again I realised how lucky we are,
To see all this without having to travel so very far.

How can people say it's grim up north?
Will all this countryside to explore,
With nature at its finest everywhere we look,
One can't help but wonder, who could ask for more?

14th June, 2020

## The Newcomer

We watched the drama about the Salisbury poisonings last night,
How terrifying for all those involved.
I couldn't help but think of Lancaster as I watched,
How our city would have shown such resolve,
As those in protective suits and gas masks,
Put up barricades to protect.

High fevers and temperatures checked.
Blood tested and nerves wrecked.

Novichok.
How ironic that it means 'newcomer',
When it made itself at home in Salisbury,
Threw its weight around like an old timer,
Spewed its evil in restaurants and streets,
Invisible and undetectable to those two sat on 'that seat',

No novice,
Not a new boy,
Not a beginner.
An expert.
Lethal.

15th June, 2020

## What the future holds

Wearing a face mask on a flight,
Sounds like a right pain,
But if it's the only way we're flying anywhere soon,
Then, I guess we shouldn't complain.

I've never been a fan of air conditioning on planes,
All those germs circulating round and round,
So maybe wearing a mask is what we should do,
Every time we leave the ground.

It's the same on public transport,
Paul wears a mask every day on the train,
Maybe this is what the future holds,
Noses and mouths will never be visible again.


16th June, 2020

## Rashford speaks from the heart

A government U-turn driven by a footballer,
Used to running rings around his opponents,
And tackling to get what he wants,
He certainly attacked this one head on.

In his compassionate open letter,
Rashford spoke from the heart, not with his feet,
And proved that to effect change,
You don't need a parliamentary seat.

He might not be lifting any silverware today,
But what he's achieved, means more than any trophy,
He's given hope...
He's given reassurance...
He's provided a lifeline.
Not many can say they've achieved that in their lifetime.

Euro 2020 is not happening this summer,
I'm sure we can live without football.
1.3 million children will not go to bed hungry this summer,
We could not have lived with the alternative.

17th June, 2020

## Football behind closed doors

Football behind closed doors,
Crowd noise with fake applause,
Every one of those seats normally taken,
Over 42,000 if I'm not mistaken.

How many of you had the same thought as me?
When you settled down to watch the match at Villa Park after tea,
Capacity there is over forty two thousand,
42,000
A similar number of people in the UK have died from Covid-19.
42,000
A full stadium.
Now empty.

During the silence at the start of the game,
It's like every single one of those plastic seats,
Represented an individual, a person, a name,
Waiting for us to pay our respects.

The debate will continue, the discussion will go on,
Do you prefer crowd switched off or do you prefer crowd switched on?
Does it really matter?
Instead, think of all those people who were with us,
Who could have been there.
But now,
Are gone.

18th June, 2020

## Dame Vera passes away

I can't help but think that Dame Vera set herself a goal,
To take part in VE Day 75.
I bet she didn't expect The Queen to quote one of her most famous lines,
In this, the most difficult of times.

Even now the words,
Of that most poignant song,
'We'll Meet Again'
Moves people to tears,
Not just veterans and widows thinking of their men,
But all of us, who weren't alive back then.

Her voice reassured those who were frightened,
She gave hope to those who were apart,
She represented home.
A remarkable woman.
The Forces' sweetheart.
An icon.

19th June, 2020

## The Summer Solstice

Today is the longest day of the year,
The Summer Solstice.
To be honest, some of the days recently have felt like the longest day,
The days when it rains and you can't spend time outside,
The days when all you really want to do is stay under the duvet and hide.

But then at other times I feel there's not enough hours to be had,
No matter how much you do, time seems to run away.
Chaucer said 'Time and tide wait for no man'
Or woman I must add.

I've got used to long days over the past few months,
Days that begin at first light,
And end in darkness, well into the night,
But it will still be a shock to the system having to set the alarm,
Even though long days seem to do no harm.

There'll be sixteen hours and thirty eight minutes of daylight today,
What will you do with your 'bonus' minutes of this long Saturday?


20th June, 2020

## Fathers' Day 2020

It's the same question every June,
Is it Fathers' or Father's Day?
Are we celebrating one father or all fathers?
To be honest it really doesn't matter but it is important to say,
Today's a day for those dads like mine who have always been there,
And who still show us the way.

I'm 'allowed' to see my dad today,
But I know some of my friends won't be as lucky as me,
We must also remember those dads who are no longer with us,
Those we are unable to hug or see.

So, Happy Fathers' Day to my dad Richard and Isla's Daddy Paul,
Happy Fathers' Day to all your dads and grandads too,
Without their love and guidance,
We really don't know what we would do.


21st June, 2020

## **Back to school**

After fifty school days at home,
Teachers will unlock their classroom doors once more,
Only this time it feels very different,
There's tape all over the floor.

After fifty school days at home,
The students will stroll through the gates just like they did before,
Not really knowing what the day has in store,
But keen to get back to normal once more.

After fifty school days at home,
Some parents will breathe a huge relieved sigh,
As their sons and daughters return to class,
But others will be anxious, fearful and perhaps will cry.

The thoughts of summer holidays are not really on our minds,
Like they usually are at this time,
We've learnt that we can't plan more than a week ahead,
Living in the moment seems the only way instead.

So, good luck to all those returning to school,
For a little bit of normality,
You will be welcomed with socially distanced open arms,
As we, once again, bring together our community.

22nd June, 2020

## **Reading Town**

I have always had a soft spot for Reading town,
Not the football club,
The people.
The place.
The place my friend Marianne calls home.

From weddings to helping out when babies arrived,
To crazy nights out for birthdays and New Year celebrations,
I've always been made to feel so welcome there,
Like a member of the family, one of the relations.

It's always felt so friendly,
So warm and full of cheer,
So, my thoughts are with their community,
As they grieve for those they hold dear.

A random but brutal act,
A community torn apart,
Three friends sat together,
So much love in their hearts.

The silences, the tributes,
The heartfelt words from family and friends,
Shows the strength of the town of Reading,
As its united heart begins to mend.

23rd June, 2020

## **<u>Back in the Classroom</u>**

Well I thought I'd forgotten how to teach,
After being away for so long,
But I managed to get through my first lesson,
And succeeded in not doing much wrong.

I didn't stand next to a student and read any of their work,
I didn't point out their spelling and punctuation mistakes,
I didn't walk over to their desk to quietly praise or reassure,
In fact I didn't move from the front which felt really fake.

Let's see what today brings,
A different set of faces,
To challenge and question and listen to as they read aloud,
Whilst encouraging them to have confidence in themselves and
make themselves feel proud.

24th June, 2020

## Heatwave

...and now the heatwave arrives,
Next week it's due to rain,
So let's make the most of it,
Rather than complain.

Make the most of sweating as soon as you get out of the shower,
Face damp as you blow dry your hair,
Putting make-up on then watching it all slide off your face,
Then the difficult task of deciding what to wear.

Then throw in the morning walk,
It's hard work in this heat,
Raspberry red burning face,
And aching overheating feet.

Thank goodness for air con, ice cream and juicy lollies,
Sand pits, hot tubs and paddling pools,
Thank goodness we live so close to the coast,
Where the welcome sea breeze helps to keep us cool.

25th June, 2020

## Covidiots Part Two

Hordes of covidiots flocked to Bournemouth beach,
Other sunbathers were lying next to them, all within close reach,
A major incident declared,
It makes us feel anxious,
And it makes us feel scared.

I really don't understand,
Why you would follow such massive crowds,
When we can never be certain,
That this virus has departed this land,
Fled our golden sands,
And been washed off our infected hands.

26th June, 2020

## Putting my Pen Down

So, with 100 poems written,
My record of lockdown is complete for now,
It seems like the right time to stop,
So today I'll take my final bow.

Thanks for all the likes,
The comments and the shares,
I've written about those I love,
My friends and family,
And I've written about people,
Who I'll never meet or see.

I started writing poems,
To document this time in history,
To record my thoughts and feelings,
A kind of therapy,
But now it's become more than that,
A gift for our daughter Isla Pearl,
Who, over the past three months,
Has become such a bright little girl.

I WILL miss it so very much,
But to be honest I'm rather glad,
I've exhausted all inspiration,
So I'm not feeling at all sad.

I've been bowled over by the reception,
Since I wrote my first poem on 20th March,
I know I've made people cry,
And I've made people laugh,
I've had dedicated followers,
Who have 'liked' even when it's naff,
I've tugged at heart strings,
And made people think,
I hope I've brought some cheer,
When you've felt like you're going to sink.

I've entered a competition,
I've had some poems published online,
I've featured in teaching newsletters,
And tweeted more than a hundred times,
Now, I'm working on a title,
And a front cover design.

You see one day I'm hoping,
To self-publish an anthology,
Full of lockdown lines,
All written in lockdown by me.

27th June, 2020

# ABOUT THE AUTHOR

Helen Davies was born in Yorkshire but has lived in Lancashire for most of her life. She is married and has a young daughter. She has been teaching English at a large secondary school in Morecambe for over twenty years. *Lockdown Lines*, Helen's first collection of poetry, was written over one hundred days during Lockdown 2020.

Printed in Great Britain
by Amazon